PERFORMANCE TESTING UNLEASHED

A Journey from Novice to Expert

Sagar Deshpande

Sagar Tambade

Preface

Performance Testing has become a most important aspect of overall development and testing life cycle. With increasing demand of responsive and stable application, a right strategy need to be defined in every stage of application development. These abstract highlights the importance of performance testing and emphasizes the need for a comprehensive approach to ensure optimal application performance. By implementing the right strategy throughout the development life cycle, organizations can effectively address performance challenges and deliver high-quality applications that meet customer expectations

Authors

Sagar Deshpande

Sagar Deshpande graduated with a degree in Electronics Engineering in 2005. He commenced his professional journey as a Software Developer at Syntel in the same year. For the past 16+ years, he has dedicated his career to Performance and Scalability Testing, with a sizable portion of it being spent at Wolters Kluwer. Currently, he leads the Center of Excellence for Performance Testing at Wolters Kluwer.

Sagar's strong technical background combined with his leadership skills has enabled him to effectively collaborate with cross-functional teams and drive innovation. He has a deep understanding of industry best practices and keeps up to date with the latest technological advancements. Sagar's genuine passion lies in assisting businesses in enhancing their customer experiences through his strategic guidance, technology assessments, and recommendations on development and performance engineering initiatives. He is well-known in his colleagues for his exceptional problem-solving abilities and his ability to identify practical solutions tailored to meet specific business needs.

In collaboration with his mentor, Ravindra Sadaphule, he co-authored the book titled "Demystifying Scalability," which was published in 2016 and can be found on Amazon. He can be reached @ Deshpande.sagar.s@gmail.com

Sagar Tambade

Sagar Tambade, an experienced software development and automation engineer, embarked on his professional journey at Worldwide Infosoft Services (WIS) & MindTree Ltd. with a focus on web application development. He has a Master's degree in Computer Applications from Pune University and has been working in the software industry for over 13+ years.

Sagar is currently working at Wolters Kluwer, focusing on performance engineering efforts to assure scalable and secure software solutions. His insatiable curiosity and commitment to learning have played a pivotal role in his professional growth, enabling him to excel within the company. Sagar deeply believes in innovative thinking and forward-looking mindset, as it consistently yielded remarkable results for him.

Sagar holds great admiration and respect for Brian Tracy, a renowned author and motivated speaker. Sagar attributes a significant transformation in his life to the profound impact of Brian Tracy's numerous books related to self-discipline. In addition to his technical prowess, Sagar is also an avid enthusiast of various disciplines. He finds great pleasure in reading articles on history, mythology, technology, travelogues, and knowledge-based topics, further nurturing his thirst for learning and self-discipline.

With a combination of technical expertise, and a passion for knowledge and unwavering drive of enthusiasm reflected in his daily work, and he remains steadfast in his commitment to pushing the boundaries of what is possible. He can be contacted via email at sagar.tambade@hotmail.com

Table of Contents

"Quality is never an accident; it is always the result of intelligent effort."

– John Ruskin

"The problem is not that testing is the bottleneck. The problem is that you don't know what's in the bottle. That's a problem that testing addresses."

— Michael Bolton, author, "Rapid Software Testing"

"It's hard enough to find an error in your code when you're looking for it; it's even harder when you've assumed your code is error-free."

— Steve McConnell, author, Code Complete

"Pretty good testing is easy to do. Excellent testing is quite hard to do."

— James Bach, founder, Satisfice

This book focus on Performance Testing and is going to talk about WHY Performance testing is required and HOW it should be done a right way.

"Testing", if you look at Google, it says - the process of evaluating how something works". However, there is no straight answer to this word in the world of Software industry as there is no single term to define it. Software testing has been categorically spelled out as.

- ✓ Black Box
- ✓ White Box
- ✓ Automation
- ✓ Manual
- ✓ Security
- ✓ Accessibility
- ✓ **Performance**
- ✓ **Load**
- ✓ **Scalability**

In this book we will talk in detail about Performance, Load and Scalability testing and would give you a tour of each of these types.

Chapter I

Functional and Non-Functional Testing

Functional and non-functional testing is a form of testing that uses different tests to ensure that your system is in line with your business plan. The testing is done as per a specification sheet. This sheet will determine how much and to what extent your system follows your business needs. Some of the functional tests that are conducted here include regression testing, system testing,

Functional Testing	Non-Functional Testing
White Box	Performance
Black Box	Security
System	Accessibility
Integration	Compatibility
User Acceptance	Data Conversion

interface testing, integration testing etc.

Non-functional testing checks how ready your system is for the end user. This is basically done to check the quality of your application. This in turn is directly linked to customer experience and customer satisfaction. Some of the non-functional tests that are usually conducted include volume testing, usability testing, resilience testing etc.

These tests all come under the broad category of performance testing services. Performance tests are the best way to ensure that your application is functioning well and is ready for your consumer. These tests are usually conducted before the website is made live. This helps in gauging the performance of the website in simulated conditions and identifying glitches.

There are several companies that will help you keep the health of your website or web application in the best form by offering performance testing services and lifecycle assurance. Lifecycle assurance is also integral to ensure that you web application is functioning optimally. Ensuring the proper functioning of your website helps you in keeping your business profitable. By availing of these services, you not only keep your website updated and abreast with the changes in the digital world but enhance consumer experience.

Performance testing services is done through several tests. Software testing is essential for any business to stay profitable. Through several tests such as load testing, endurance testing, configuration testing, spike testing etc., the behavior of the website is checked, and problems are identified. By getting these tests done before launching your website or new web application you can save energy and costs on damage repairs and maintenance

Chapter II

Performance Testing

Term "Performance" here, has no relation or association with act or presentation. Here it is used to measure a Software or a website or an application responsiveness to user actions. Use actions can be any activity performed by a person who is using the application or website. User and its action are very important terms here as you learn more about Performance

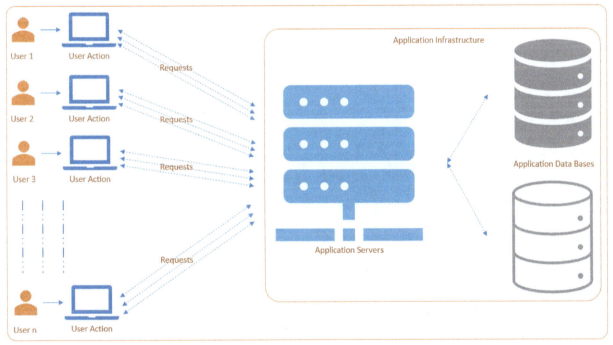

Testing.

It is the base of HOW you will be planning and performing your testing methodologies for application or website under test. Performance Testing in a very simple terms is a non-functional testing technique with standard method or process through which one can determine or measure application behavior in terms of responsiveness and stability under various workload. Many times, performance testing has also been termed as Load Testing that mainly because one can only evaluate an application performance under load if it must be done in a right way. Load is nothing but the number of requests pushed through any resource for specified period. In the following chapters we will learn various methods based on different objectives and testing requirements. In next chapter we would talk in detail on these objectives.

Chapter III

Performance Testing Objectives

Business or Product should clearly define performance testing objectives for their application(s). It is very important that Load Testing objectives are defined clearly at the beginning itself before starting the project. Once you understand the application, you should be able to draw your needs and requirements to define Load testing objectives. The objectives should answer "Why" part of Application's Load testing needs. You should be convinced with "Why" part before proceeding with actual work.

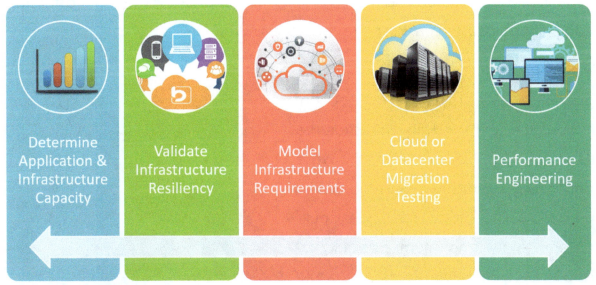

With clear objectives, vision would be clear and hence activities around load testing can be defined and planned accordingly. Lot of time it is seen that people just take load test executions without even knowing if the result would really of any help to conclude with the available data/information. When objectives are not clear, there is no direction to the work that gets performed and hence conclusions won't be valid

Objectives should address all the Load testing requirements of application under test. If you miss to define any objective, it can lead to a gap which can have ripple effect on overall application performance and scalability plan which in-turn affect Organization with its reputation. Performance Testing objectives help drive the approach to test and provides direction for capturing the requirement for test data, volume, test infrastructure and tools to use. We have categorized top 5 Performance Testing objectives as below.

1. Determine Application and Infrastructure Capacity

This is a very common objective for any performance testing team for any application that needs performance testing to be done. For any application, it is required to determine the limiting factors of various infrastructure components its uses in addition to the code limitations.

While working towards this objective, one must understand the application, its architecture and its infrastructure with all the moving parts. While performing a load test with increasing user load (Step load test), we could determine the maximum capacity of application or infrastructure could handle. Capacity in terms of users or requests.

It requires a lot of analysis to determine the cause of limiting factor, whether it is at app layer, or server layer or at DB layer. One should also perform a detailed root cause analysis to determine what actions can be performed to level up the capacity of these each component. Also, to determine various scaling ways that application or infrastructure could support with increasing load demands in future. That would provide critical information to business for make crucial decisions.

2. Validate Infrastructure Resiliency

Infrastructure Resiliency is capability of the infrastructure to withstand consistent high load for longer duration of the time along with its capabilities to quickly recover from the errored state. A resilient infrastructure could result in high availability for an application which is a default requirement for any business in today's world.

Think of an outage in WhatsApp that impacted all their customers who couldn't use the chat App for hours which became some news very quickly. While talking about this example one must take into consideration the user base who can quickly switch apps if one is not working out for them or having constant issues. These Gen z users wouldn't think twice to move out and use something which is more relevant and reliable to them.

Similarly, an outage that stopped MS Teams to work properly. These outages once become public can cause huge revenue loss to businesses and potential of losing big customers. A client would rather pay higher value to a stable application than losing out their revenue due to an unstable application.

Validation of Infrastructure Resiliency is done by taking Soak test or Longevity test or one can call it an Endurance test. These tests ideally should be taken for longer duration with consistent or varying load depending on the application usage pattern and server reset cycle. These tests capture application and importantly infrastructure behavior during the test to determine potential issues that may occur and would know the reasons for the same so that those issues can be avoided in production.

3. Model Infrastructure Requirements

Infrastructure cost is usually around 25% of overall business operation cost and though every business strives to save the cost and look for options, no one would like to take the risk of losing customer due to an outage. The fear is mainly due to lack of required information and proven execution plan that would

provide an assurance to businesses to stay available at any given time. There are methods and techniques through which this can be achieved.

Every business and application have a unique usage pattern that is based on the nature of business, geo locations and user personas. However, each has a defined peak load pattern for a set period. Though businesses need to be prepared to support that identified peak load pattern, they are not required to maintain the infrastructure throughput the day/months/year to support such high load volume.

Let's take a very familiar to all example of an e-commerce website that always has a peak during their Big SALE period. Though they do have regular SALE throughout the year based on various events or occasions, there is always a BIG SALE in a year. Most of the time a Load and workflow pattern is known for New and Existing customers that are going to be put on their system.

Techniques of using this information and corelating it with the infrastructure requirement is Infrastructure Modelling. Determining the unit requirement for each infrastructure component or resource to formulating it into the load requirements throughout the year to provide a validated Infrastructure requirement plan is a Model. This model could be different for each application and not one size fits all, however, the process to generate and exercise the model would be same.

4. Cloud or Datacenter Migration

A lot of companies are migrating their applications to cloud and App services mainly for 3 reasons that are; Low maintenance, Cost Effective, High Availability. However, it is very crucial to determine the best technology, components and SKUs to use while migrating to Cloud.

In terms of Application performance, every migrating product or application expect similar or better performance on cloud. However, a lot of time to achieve the same, they end up configuring very high SKUs for the cloud resources that makes their infrastructure cost to go very high and it becomes an overhead than reducing the cost.

While performing such migration, one must have an approach after studying the overall infrastructure architecture and its requirements based on the data and information captured from existing Data center performance tests. These tests would provide directions towards deciding the best configuration for infrastructure components and to choose the right components in the infrastructure. The tests are also required to plan on the newly setup cloud infrastructure to further fine tune to use it optimally. Few more steps are also required to determine auto scaling configurations to effectively use cloud setup.

5. Performance Engineering

A development team while working on a performance issue have a very limited perspective of identifying the root cause. Performance issues are not always straight forward and required a lot of analytical skills to dig deeper into the generated data to find the actual root cause. Moreover, developers most of the time doesn't have a complete visibility beyond their development scope and sometimes also won't have visibility in the infrastructure components that are executing

their designed and developed code. While the issues are usually getting surfaced under load, it is mostly impossible for a dev team to reproduce the issues even if they believe they are fixed. However, a performance tester does have all these insights.

If you have access to a complete infrastructure, code, DB and APM tools, it opens a huge opportunity to trigger comprehensive root cause analysis of performance issues observed during your tests. Performance Engineering is to correlate all the captured information during and after execution to formulate or articulate a convincing theory based on data and information on to WHY an issue has surfaced. Though the theory has data to back, it needs to be validated repeating the tests.

Performance Engineering covers Code Profiling, SQL Profiling, Dump Analysis, Designing, Planning and Executing various experimental tests to understand the issue and then look for possible fix.

Chapter IV

Performance Testing vs Performance Engineering

A process in which an objective is to determine or identify capacity or limiting factor of the infrastructure under test for an application by putting various load levels is mainly done in Performance Testing. To understand what kind of infrastructure or resources or its configuration is required to sustain certain load level or to be able to handle peak load of the application, the system is pushed with different load levels and study the behavior and impact on each resource such that a limiting factor is  identified. These then put into a calculation to estimate required resources and their optimum configuration at any given point of time. This is to identify optimum set of processes to effectively use the infrastructure for a given application behavior for anticipated user actions and usage pattern for its peak.

A process through which a detailed analysis is done to determine the root cause of a performance or scalability problem is Performance Engineering. Performance Engineering is a vast subject where to understand the problem, one must understand the implementation and business around it. A solution to a problem also needs to adhere to the requirements than just solving it in isolation. Without impacting the actual behavior of the user behavior, an issue needs to be fixed. Another aspect to look while performing a root cause analysis is to determine where the actual problem roots are, is it at the application level or at infrastructure level. If it is at infrastructure level, which area or resources are limiting is a key to come up with a desired solution. Sometimes, the solution could be very straight forward like breaking a loop in

the code OR changing the throttling limitations of a resources OR changing the configuration of a DB to avoid timeouts. However, most of the time, problems are very complex and hard to identify and the solution to it could be challenging and complex

enough, we would need many cycles of the testing efforts to determine the optimum solution. This end-to-end process to identify the problem and then to determine the optimum solution to it is a part of Performance Engineering. In certain instances, code profiling is required to be done to determine code level issues where probes are added to the code and behavior of that code snippet is studied to find options for optimization. To prove an analytical solution works, sometimes you may need to do Performance Testing.

Both these are parallel stream of activities that needed to be performed to find effective and optimum way to solve a problem. Remember that Performance Engineering is not a straightforward process and requires time and efforts to address any performance issue. Situation, Severity and Criticality of an issue determines the path of finding a fix.

If business requires a quick fix for a severe production issue, a long process of performance engineering may not help and a quick fix to check where infrastructure scaling would help is an answer for that moment, however, to avoid it in future, one should do a root cause analysis through a process of Performance Engineering for a permanent fix.

Performance Testing	Performance Engineering
Usage Pattern Analysis	Test Result & Errors Analysis
Scripting & Test Execution	Server Dump Analysis
Result Consolidation	Database Stats Analysis
Result Analysis	Database Tuning & Optimization
Defect Management	APM Tools Analysis
Summation & Reporting	Code Profiling

Also, all problems are not required to be taken for Performance Engineering, like, in situations where performance impact is low and its likelihood is limited and known with spending for additional resources is an effective way to solve a problem than putting efforts to identify and fix through analysis, a wiser decision has to be taken accordingly as Performance Engineering may need development team and their Architect teams time to work with a performance engineer for finding a better fix.

Chapter V

Evolving World Web & Need of Performance Testing

World Web has changed the way software applications are being used. In recent past, software or applications or tools are mostly desktop based where performance of it is very much limited and subjective to the client's machine and their Internet connections. Load testing is not at all required for such

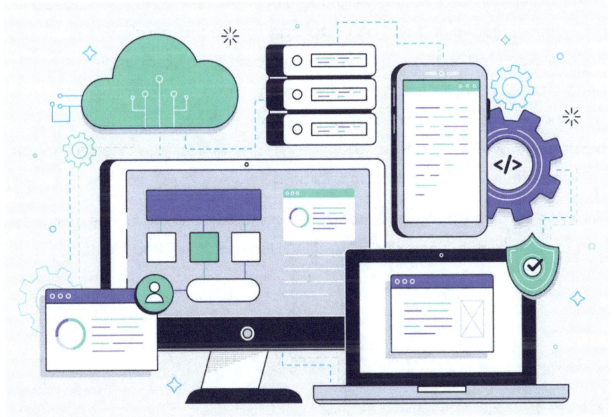

applications as the user are very limited. Either a single user or a group of small users on LAN. Performance Engineering practices and processes were mainly used to correct user action performance through code profiling and network is simulated though a software simulator to mimic client internet connection providers and types. With evolving Internet bandwidth and ranges, browsing speed and data transfer is no longer a problem and has changed the way solutions being provided to consumers and users. Applications are required to be online and available through internet that has migrated almost all desktop-based applications and tools to a service-based websites. With this change, a need of Performance Testing or Load testing has emerged. Users would not like to wait and see a processing icon for their actions on the screen and needs a quick result. These expectations cannot be addressed through a conventional way of automation testing and needed a special performance testing to be performed.

With the introduction of Cloud Infrastructure where businesses have started to find solutions to save cost and a standard and managed infrastructure solution, Performance Testing has become a crucial gate keeper. As through performance testing, effective and optimum cloud configuration could be determined, businesses started investing a lot on Performance Testing. Some businesses have a mandate for a dev team to test their code through performance test before it goes to final build.

Adhering to all these business needs without compromising user experience and expectations, business started drafting Non-Functional Requirements.

Chapter VI

Understand Non-Functional Requirements (NFRs)

Requirements gathering is a crucial process that enables the success of a system or software project to be assessed. In software world, requirements are typically categorized as Functional and Non-functional requirements.

Functional Requirements

Functional requirements describe what a system or application should do, specifying its features, functionalities, and behavior. These requirements define the system's intended capabilities and how it should respond to specific inputs or actions. They are typically expressed as user stories, use cases, or specific system behavior descriptions.

Using functional requirements actual outputs are compared against expected behaviors. This provides a clearer overall picture than testing individual modules in isolation. Interactions between modules are frequently the points where errors occur, this testing is covered through functional requirements.

Non-functional Requirements

Non-functional requirements define the qualities or characteristics of a system, such as performance, reliability, usability, security, scalability, maintainability, and availability. These requirements focus on how the system should perform or behave rather than what it should do. Non-functional requirements are often related to the system's performance, efficiency, and user experience.

Non-functional requirements help assessing application properties that aren't critical to functionality but contribute to the end-user experience. Here performance and reliability aspects of non-functional testing which are associated with load aren't functional components of a software system but can certainly make or break the user experience.

Why are functional and non-functional requirements important to the business?

Functional Requirements	Non-functional Requirements
Meeting User Expectations Functional requirements ensure that the system or application meets the users' needs and expectations by providing specific features and functionalities. This helps in satisfying customer requirements and increasing user satisfaction.	**System Performance and Reliability** Non-functional requirements, particularly performance requirements, ensure that the system can handle the expected workload and provide a seamless user experience. Reliability requirements ensure that the system operates consistently and minimizes downtime, enhancing customer trust and loyalty.
Functional aspects They speak about what a product must do or have	**Scalability and Growth** Non-functional requirements related to scalability and maintainability help businesses plan for future growth and ensure that the system can handle increased user loads and data volumes. This allows for business expansion without significant system redesign or performance issues.
The requirements stated by the end user These are the requirements that the end user specifically demands as basic facilities that the system should	**Regulatory Compliance** Non-functional requirements, such as security and privacy requirements, ensure that the system adheres to relevant regulations and industry

offer. All these functionalities need to be necessarily incorporated into the system as a part of the contract. They are basically the requirements stated by the user which one can see directly in the final product,	standards. This helps the business avoid legal and financial penalties and maintain a trustworthy reputation.
Example 1) Authentication of user whenever he/she logs into the system. 2) System shutdown in case of a cyber-attack. 3) A Verification email is sent to user whenever he/she registers for the first time on some software system.	Example 1) Emails should be sent with a latency of no greater than 12 hours from such an activity. 2) The processing of each request should be done within 10 seconds 3) The site should load in 3 seconds when the number of simultaneous users are > 10000 4) Application servers should be utilizing < 60% avg. CPU

How to capture NFRs for Performance Testing

To collect non-functional requirements specifically for performance testing, consider the following approaches:

1. Stakeholder Interviews: Conduct interviews with project stakeholders, including business owners, users, and technical teams. Ask questions about expected performance, response time, concurrent user load, and any specific performance-related concerns they may have.

2. Performance Workshops: Organize workshops with relevant stakeholders to discuss and gather non-functional requirements related to performance. Facilitate discussions around performance expectations, scalability needs, and any critical performance factors.

3. Analyze Existing Documentation: Review existing project documentation, such as business requirements, technical specifications, and architectural diagrams. Look for any performance-related information or requirements that have already been documented.

designed by freepik

4. Collaborative Meetings: Engage in collaborative meetings with the development team, architects, and infrastructure experts. Discuss system design, technical constraints, and any known performance-related challenges or considerations.

5. Prototypes and Proof of Concepts: Develop prototypes or proof of concepts to demonstrate specific performance aspects of the system. Use these demonstrations to collect feedback and gather non-functional requirements related to performance.

6. Performance Baseline Analysis: Analyze the existing system's performance and collect data on current performance metrics. Identify areas for improvement and gather non-functional requirements to enhance performance.

7.   External Benchmarks and Standards: Refer to industry benchmarks, standards, and best practices for performance requirements. These external references can help in setting performance targets and determining acceptable performance levels.

It is recommended to document and validate the collected non-functional requirements with the stakeholders to ensure a shared understanding and alignment with their expectations.

Chapter VII

Choosing a Right Testing Tool

Selecting the right tool for load testing purposes is critical for ensuring accurate performance assessments of your software application. By following the step-by-step approach outlined in this write-up, you can identify a load testing tool that aligns with your objectives, offers the necessary features and capabilities, and fits within your budget. Conduct thorough evaluations and consider factors such as protocol support, user load handling, scripting capabilities, reporting, scalability.

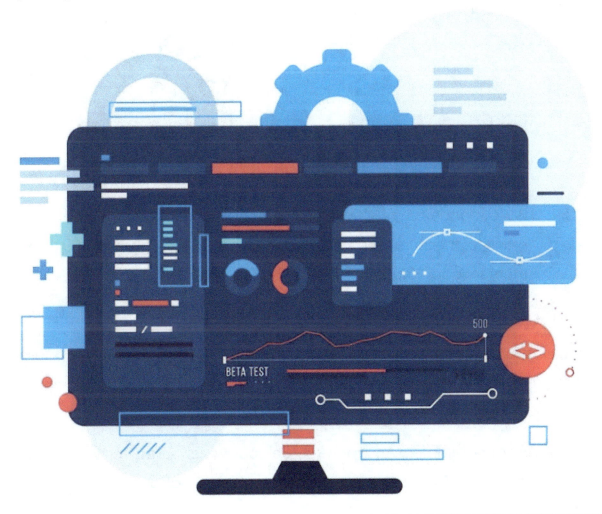

To conduct effective load testing, it is essential to choose the right tool that aligns with your requirements. here, we will discuss a step-by-step approach for identifying the appropriate tool for load testing purposes in performance testing.

Step 1

Define Your Load Testing Objectives Before beginning the tool selection process, it is important to clearly define your load testing objectives so while finalizing the tool, the expectations/objectives would be evaluated accordingly, to start with following are some of the factors to consider

1. Expected user load: Determine the anticipated number of users accessing your application simultaneously.

2. Types of transactions: Identify the specific actions or transactions users will perform, such as browsing, searching, purchasing, or data entry.

3. Performance metrics: Determine the key performance indicators you want to measure, such as response times, throughput, CPU usage, memory consumption, or network latency.

Step 2

Research Available Load Testing Tools Conduct thorough research to identify the load testing tools available in the market. Consider both commercial and open-source options. Some popular load testing tools include:

1. Apache JMeter: An open-source tool widely used for load testing, capable of simulating various protocols and platforms.

2. LoadRunner: A commercial tool offering a comprehensive set of features for load testing.

3. Gatling: An open-source tool written in Scala, providing high-performance load testing capabilities.

4. Blaze Meter: A cloud-based load testing platform that integrates with various open-source tools.

5. Locust: An open-source tool known for its simplicity and scalability.

Step 3

Evaluate Tool Features and Capabilities Once you have identified potential load testing tools, evaluate them based on the following factors:

1. Protocol support: Ensure that the tool supports the protocols used by your application, such as HTTP, HTTPS, WebSockets, or SOAP.

2. Simultaneous user support: Verify that the tool can handle the anticipated number of simultaneous users.

3. Scripting capabilities: Assess the tool's scripting capabilities, as scripts are used to simulate user interactions and define test scenarios.

4. Reporting and analysis: Check if the tool provides detailed reports and analysis of performance metrics.

5. Integration options: Consider whether the tool integrates well with your existing development and testing environment.

6. Ease of use: Evaluate the tool's user interface, ease of configuration, and the learning curve required to operate it effectively.

Step 4

Consider Performance and Scalability Load testing tools themselves must be capable of handling the desired load. Consider the performance and scalability aspects of the load testing tools you are evaluating. Ensure that the tool can generate the required load without becoming a bottleneck itself.

Step 5

Community and Support Evaluate the tool's community and support ecosystem. A strong user community, active forums, and readily available documentation can provide valuable resources when encountering issues or seeking guidance.

Step 6

Cost Considerations Finally, consider the cost implications. Compare the licensing models and pricing structures of commercial tools, including factors such as upfront costs, maintenance fees, and additional support requirements. For open-source tools, evaluate the associated infrastructure costs and any limitations in terms of enterprise support.

Chapter VIII

Workload modeling

Workload modeling is a critical aspect of performance testing as it allows testers to simulate real-world user behavior and system usage patterns. By creating an accurate representation of how users interact with the application or system, workload modeling enables testers to assess the system's

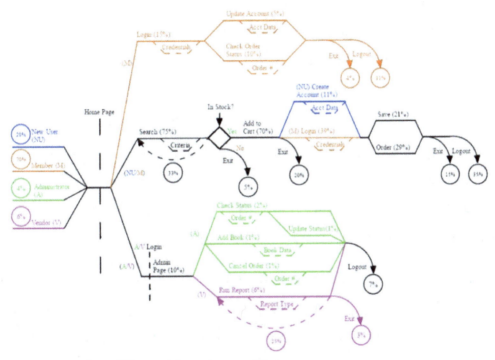

performance under different load conditions.

This includes factors such as the number of concurrent users, the frequency and duration of user actions, and the variability in user behavior. By incorporating these elements into the workload model, testers can gain valuable insights into how the system will perform in production and identify any performance bottlenecks or scalability issues that need to be addressed.

One of the key benefits of workload modeling is its ability to predict the system's performance under different load scenarios. By simulating various user activities, concurrency levels, and data volumes, testers can estimate performance metrics such as response time, throughput, and resource utilization. This information is invaluable for capacity planning, resource allocation, and identifying any performance limitations that could impact the system's ability to handle expected user loads. Workload modeling helps organizations make informed decisions about infrastructure scaling, identifying the need for additional resources or optimizations to ensure the system can handle the anticipated load.

Additionally, workload modeling aids in risk identification by subjecting the system to various load scenarios. By carefully designing the workload model, testers can uncover potential performance issues and vulnerabilities that might arise under specific conditions. By proactively identifying these risks, organizations can take steps to address them before the system is deployed in a production environment. This helps ensure a smooth user experience and reduces the likelihood of performance-related incidents once the system is in use. Workload modeling plays a vital role in mitigating risks and enhancing the overall performance and reliability of the system.

To summarize, workload modeling is an essential component of performance testing. It enables testers to simulate real-world user behavior, predict system performance under different load scenarios, and identify performance bottlenecks and scalability issues. By accurately representing user activities, concurrency levels, and data volumes, organizations can make informed decisions about resource allocation, capacity planning, and risk mitigation. Workload modeling ultimately contributes to delivering a high-performing and reliable system that meets user expectations and business requirements.

Chapter IX

Test Strategy and Planning

To being a performance testing project for any application, it is always advisable to start with building your Test Strategy and a Plan. The test strategy talks about the "How" part of the process that defines the approach to achieve required test objectives.

To build a Test Strategy, one should know answers for below basic questions.

- Business objectives for Performance Testing of an Application under test. A "Why" part of it.
- Critical business scenarios or Production usage pattern
- What are various User personas of an application under test
- What kind of Test Data or Data Volume and its data integrity is required to perform desired scenarios
- Do business have defined KPIs

Each of the above is in some or the other form a part of NFRs. However, as a performance tester, you need to make sure these are captured well with validated information available. Test Strategy which is a key that defines the approach must fed with the right information to get the desired results. If the information is superlative, the results generated through the tests may show false positive outputs.

Test Strategy and Planning can be drafted into below listed items that you could use as a template.

Test Objectives

Clearly defined test objectives are very crucial as it would decide which types of test methodologies that you would apply to achieve the same. Also, the test objectives define the kind of information required from stakeholders or production APM tools to design the tests. Test objectives should be drafted and accordingly all other testing practices should be mapped together.

Test Scope

Scope of the test that defines the boundaries and scope out some of the areas

which are not in application control such as third-party APIs and applications that are used for any specific function. Scope also talks about efforts in building the test data volume and the scope of development and architect teams' involvement to do so. To draft the scope well, one should properly understand and study Application and Infrastructure Architecture. It would be also wise to document the analytical expectations and involvement. As for a short project committing to provide the root cause could kill the timelines, for a longer project it makes sense to get involved into deep dive analysis with stakeholders to provide end to end solution pertaining to performance test objectives.

Scenarios to Test

End to End business transactions and user actions creates a scenario. For a Transaction based application or an API or Services based application,

scenario could be a single API, or a group of APIs logically grouped together to cover a specific user action. Every transaction or request that need to be covered usually need to map with user actions on the screen. Most of the time, this information is captured by studying production logs and its usage pattern, however, for new

applications, BAs should be approached to get this information. Apart from the transactions and requests to cover, it is very important to know their throughput that is required to be achieved. Transaction numbers should be achieved to conclude the capacity.

Test Data

For performance test to execute in a right way, right set of test data is required. Test data in terms of volume and data integrity and data complexity should be built. There are two ways – Use Production data after scrubbing the sensitive PI data OR build the data from scratch. Building data from scratch takes a lot of time and efforts. Also, to maintain integrity and data complexity, it is advisable to use user action automation script or load test script to generate the data the way users are generating it on production. This process would take months to populate large set of data.

So, wherever possible, it would be quick to use Production Database directly to carry out performance testing. In the Strategy, if production DB is planned to be used, scrubbing techniques and responsibilities should be defined clearly. In case, data is to be built from scratch, approach for the same should be drafted with timelines. Also, remember that the process to build the data from scratch slows down after certain data volume due to application slowness that may be observed for growing data sets. So, mindfully create timelines of the data generation. In addition to test data generation, preparing Input test data for the scripts should also be planned. For Production scrubbed copies,

process to filter out the input test data to cover required set of tenants, entities and users with roles should be defined. In similar way, for the generated test data, process to capture definite set of inputs should be drafted. Remember that, sometime even when you receive a production scrub copy, you may be required to generate data on top of that to create desired volume to test future state of the anticipated data volume. Sometime, this is also true for scenarios where impact of data growth is one of the objectives to test. Such scenarios and requirements should be drafted clearly in this Test Data strategy.

Performance Test Infrastructure

Identifying and defining the infrastructure to do Performance Testing is very critical as it could screw up the results if not choose, set and configured properly. Infrastructure is backbone of Performance Testing. In the Strategy document, one should specify what kind and scale of infrastructure is required.

Objective of the test drive infrastructure requirement in performance testing. For a scaled down version of test cycles, a small infrastructure is required. For a test matching projected load, an infrastructure of production grade and scale would be needed. Similarly, to identify limiting factors of any component, properly scaled component would be required for

testing. Once the scenarios and scripts are built, it is getting tested on various infrastructure setup to achieve various performance testing objectives. Note that, no matter how scale down or scaled up infrastructure you are using, you should always validate the configuration of each of the infrastructure component to match it with production. Finding optimum configuration would be the step ahead, however, aligning it with production to begin with is very important to get a valid baseline of application under test. While building a strategy, you may begin with the infrastructure that is getting used and built in for any other testing purposes like manual or automation testing. This would majorly be scoped only for checking the scripting and getting hands on to application and its scenarios. This would also be since building an environment or infrastructure could take time. However, an isolated Performance Test environment must be asked for better results. In case a shared infrastructure is provided, a test or any activity being carried out while Performance test is getting executed could screw the results invalidating the test.

Test Approach

Test Approach is a heart of test strategy. This section describes how we plan to achieve test objectives on the given infrastructure with defined scenarios and workload model and on the planned test data. Approach starts with scripting techniques to be used, test tool to be considered for testing and the way executions are planned. Approach consists of key activities that would defines the best possible way to execute the test on the application to achieve desired results. Phasing out of the scopes and outputs can also be a part of Approach. Usually, POCs and executing the lower load test after scripting it on test environment is considered or drafted as a first phase of the approach where the deliverable is to  finalize tools and techniques to script and test an application. This phase is also mostly used to define KPIs if those are not already provided by business. In case those are provided, those can get validated with low load test in this phase. A lot of time unrealistic KPIs if provided gets flagged out for review and corrections. In this phase, data generation requirements and approach also get finalized. Once the base is setup with first phase, next phases usually are the replica of each other where after establishing Baseline, regression and other test cycles are carried out. These phases are listed in a very high level since these phases are depending on the output of Phase 1.

Acceptance Criteria / Exit Criteria

While defining the approach and testing methods, it is also very crucial to define Agreements and criteria in your strategy. Each project has a delivery and timeline scope associated with it, that get extended or renewed based on features and solutions, however, for each of the requirement, stakeholders should be expecting a definite outcome. For Performance Testing, this definite

outcome is not always quantifiable and hence it would always be better to draft these expectations as Exit criteria very clearly in the strategy itself.

Chapter X

Scripting – the right way

Scripting - Visual Studio Load Testing

 Before you start recording or coding your performance test scripts, take some time to think about what information you want to get from your scripts and what information you want to get from your monitoring tools. For any information you want your scripts to provide, you're probably going to want a timer of some sort.

We can look at both the individual transaction times as well as the aggregate times across scenarios. If you need aggregate numbers, it's normally better to get the information from aggregate timers than by coming up with the numbers yourself. Many times, when we try to aggregate the numbers

ourselves, we perform operations on the numbers that make the results no longer valid. For example, you can't average ninetieth-percentiles of each scenario to get the ninetieth-percentile for the run. If you want that, you should aggregate your timers. Otherwise, you'll need to go back to the raw data and build your aggregate numbers from there.

Once you know what you need to measure in your scripts, you've got one last thing to think about before you start recording. Do you want to document the scripts you create and how do you do that? However, there are several factors that can get me to document my performance test scripts:

- If there are several scripts, it can be a lot to keep track of and remember.
- If the scripts are complex and require a lot of attention to detail during creation, it can be helpful to reference something when maintaining them.
- If you need to maintain the scripts over a long period of time, it can be nice to have something to jog your memory.
- And finally, if you have more than one or two people working in the scripts, it can be difficult to coordinate across the team.

Once you're ready to start developing the scripts, with most tools you'll begin with a recording. After you record, that's when the real work starts. At a minimum, you'll want to go in and add any additional timers and you'll want to update your think times. You may also need to add custom correlations for values within the script, or you may need to parameterize variables for data you read in from various data sources.

For some applications, you may need to go into the code and

remove any unneeded or unwanted posts or downloads. Those can include cascading style sheets, JavaScript files, images and other transactions depending on the goals of your tests. For many web-client applications, you may also need to add custom function calls or write custom code using a toolkit of some sort.

Regardless of what you must do, consider creating a scripting checklist. Something that reminds you of everything that needs to be done after you record your scripts. It can include some of the scripting tasks mentioned above, or it could include process steps like notifying team members, uploading final files or checking your scripts into source control. Whatever you find you need to do on a regular basis, it can sometimes be helpful to give yourself a reminder. When working in a team, it can also be helpful to track the status of your scripts somewhere that the entire team can access. That way everyone knows what work still needs to be done and where they can jump in to provide any support.

VSTS load testing tool is usually being leveraged for both WCF and Web-based application to mimic production like load.

Script structure

Any script should be maintained in following structure.

- Initialize section - For data source handling.

- Business Transaction - It depicts the UI activity

- Transaction - It depict URL hit.

Code Review

Business Transaction and Transactions should have proper Prefix to categorize it as Business transaction and transaction.

Test script should be executed for single user prior of merging it in TFS solution.

Real user simulation through Load test | Reduced Login approach

Problem

VSTS spawns' threads for each iteration and each thread has its own user context | properties. VSTS has option to maintain login sessions as much as total number of virtual users being used in test or total number of iterations going to be executed during test. However, it does not provide a support to simulate intermediate user logins and multiple iterations operations with same session with happens in real world.

Approach

Solution which can help to share sessions within user defined thread count or iterations. To make that possible Visual studio load test plugin has implemented to keep track of users and their iterations to be executed by same session.

What is plug-in?

In computing, a plug-in (or plugin, extension, or add-on / addon) is a software component that adds a specific feature to an existing software application. When an application supports plug-ins, it enables customization. We implemented user-based plugin that help scenario execution to decide whether to do a login or mimic a login by using a saved token.

User Based plug-in Implementation Steps

```
public class UserBasedLoadTestPlugin : ILoadTestPlugin
{
```

- Create a class that implements ILOADTESTPLUGIN

- Define a variable that decides how many iterations needs to be executed for a given scenario and define a dictionary that holds

```
int PortalSearchMaxIterationCountPerUser = 6;
int PortalUploadMaxIterationCountPerUser = 3;

Dictionary<int, int> PortalUploadUserBasedCount = new Dictionary<int, int>();
Dictionary<int, int> PortalSearchUserBasedCount = new Dictionary<int, int>();
```

userid and count of iterations to execute.

- In the TestStarting event write the logic to check whether to login or not for each scenario.

- Scenario name should be the test class name of that scenario

- based on user id, the count is managed

```
private void TestStarting(object source, TestStartingEventArgs testStartingEventArgs)
{
    lock (this)
    {
        boolean flag = false;
        if (testStartingEventArgs.TestName == "OpenReturnTest")
        {
            if (OpenReturnUserBasedCount.ContainsKey(testStartingEventArgs.UserContext.UserId) &&
                OpenReturnUserBasedCount[testStartingEventArgs.UserContext.UserId] != 0)
            {
                flag = false;

                if (OpenReturnUserBasedCount[testStartingEventArgs.UserContext.UserId] == OpenReturnMaxIterationCountPerUser)
                {
                    flag = true;
                    OpenReturnUserBasedCount[testStartingEventArgs.UserContext.UserId] = 0;
                }
                OpenReturnUserBasedCount[testStartingEventArgs.UserContext.UserId] += 1;
                //else
                //{
                //    flag = false;
                //}
            }
            else
            {
                OpenReturnUserBasedCount.Remove(testStartingEventArgs.UserContext.UserId);
                OpenReturnUserBasedCount.Add(testStartingEventArgs.UserContext.UserId, 1);
                flag = true;
            }
        }
```

- A flag is set in the test context which then be used in the test method

- in a test method, login is done based on the flag that gets its value in the plugin

- once the login is done, token and required data is stored in the

```
foreach (KeyValuePair<string, object> keyValuePair in m_loadTest.Context)
{
    testStartingEventArgs.TestContextProperties.Add(keyValuePair.Key, keyValuePair.Value);
}
testStartingEventArgs.TestContextProperties.Add("UserId", testStartingEventArgs.UserContext.UserId);
testStartingEventArgs.TestContextProperties.Add("doLogin", flag);
```

dictionary which then be used in the else part where login is mimicked.

```
[TestMethod()]
public void AccountsReceivable_SF()
{
    try
    {
        Boolean doLogin = (Boolean)_testContext.Properties["doLogin"];
        int virtualuserId = (int)_testContext.Properties["UserId"];

        CCH.LoadTest.TokenInput tokenInput = new CCH.LoadTest.TokenInput();

        if (doLogin)
        {

        Initialization

        Dashboard_login

        }
        else
        {
            ElsePart
        }
```

- The plugin then can be added to any load test file that implements this approach of reduced login.

```
3-Mix_Practice_FirmWise(1000U)
   Scenarios
   Counter Sets
   Run Settings
      Run Settings2 [Active]
   Load Test Plug-ins
      UserBasedLoadTestPlugin
```

MODULAR APPROACH IN SCRIPTING IN VSTS

Modular approach is implemented in scripts to avoid write/update same code at many places. Common functionalities are written in one place and can use them in different scripts. Suppose there are four scripts for any project with same login, home page requests. Why to write these common areas multiples times in all scripts? This automatically reduces the time to update scripts with no errors/mistakes.

Implementation

Extension method approach in C# is used to implement modularization in scripts. Extension methods allow you to inject additional methods without modifying, deriving or recompiling the original class, struct or interface. Extension methods can be added to your own custom class, .NET framework classes, or third-party classes or interfaces.

- Define one public static method in static class
- First parameter is the class for which extension method has been written
- can pass any number of parameters with any return type

When we create any new web script, webtest class gets inherited. That means current scripts can have all the properties of webtest class. Modularization in scripts is nothing but common method writing at one place can have accessed them anywhere in webtest /class inheriting webtest class or in any other class with webtest object.

E.g., all scripts have login as the common functionality. Follow below steps to implement modular approach for login part

- Define LaunchLogin method in any public static class.
- Set return type of that method 'IEnumerable<WebTestRequest>'. GetRequestEnumerator method from script has this return type with yield.
- Pass first parameter to this method as 'this webtest' and can add additional parameters like username, password etc.
- Method defined in any static function

```
public static IEnumerable<WebTestRequest> LaunchLogin(this WebTest webtest, LoggedUserContext userContextData)
{
```

- Method accessed from script

```
foreach (var webrequest in this.LaunchLogin(userContextData)) yield return webrequest
```

- All the webtest properties can be accessed in this extension

```
var document2 = new HtmlAgilityPack.HtmlDocument();
document2.LoadHtml(webtest.LastResponse.BodyString);
if (webtest.Name == "ProcedureAddWorkpaper")
{
    parentNodes2 = document2.DocumentNode.SelectNodes(".//div[@data-type]");
}
```

method with 'webtest.' Syntax

Scripting – Load Runner

Recording function enables you to specify what information to record and which functions to use when generating a Vuser script, by selecting a recording level.

- Protocol – There are multiple protocols available as per business need whereas few popular protocols are mentioned below for the reference
  - Web HTTP/HTTPS - This protocol needs to be selected for Web application
  - .Net Protocol - This should be selected for WCF application
- Recording for web-based application, best option to record scenario is **HTML Based Script**. With Advanced option, below listed options should be selected to capture URLs rather than only user actions and to ignore non-HTML generated elements.

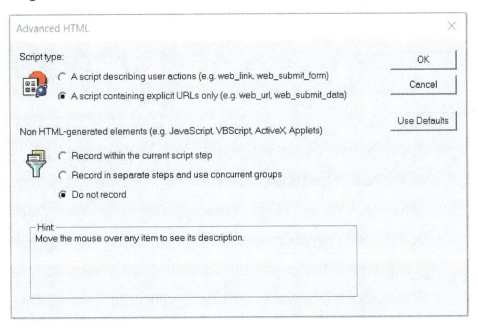

- Here you can set the script generation preferences by setting the scripting language and options Select C language to generate the Vuser script

Script Structure

Any script should be maintained in following structure

- **Vuser_init** – this action should contain Business Logic which should get execute only once per vuser. You can add LR parameter here to attach pre/postfix to the transaction. Like 'lr_save_string("XS", "ClientType");'

- **Login** – Login should be in different and separate action so can be control during execution

- **User actions** – Main user workflows/BT's should be in separate action. You can have multiple actions for different BTs. If you want some control on user actions to be performed in percent wise, then that should be in  different actions. For example, Scenario File Operations having actions like upload and download file. And it is expected to complete 70% operation for upload and 30% operations for download then there must be 2 different actions one is for upload, and another is for download. If throughput of A is 10 then upload will execute in7 iterations and 3 will be for download.

- **Logout** – Logout also should be maintained in different and separate actions o **Vuser_end** – This action contains all closing connection if you're opening during vuser_init

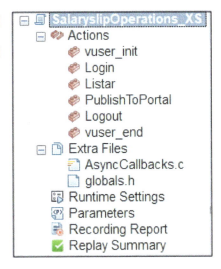

Code Review

- Scenario level transaction and Business Transaction should have proper Prefix to categorize it as scenario and Business transaction
- Test script should be executed for single user prior of uploading to performance center

Real user simulation through Load test | Reduced Login approach

Objective – To simulate intermediate user logins and multiple iterations operations with same session which happens in real world

Solution –

- First to track Iteration number and Max iteration count per login, define two parameters for IterationNumber and MaxIterationCount-- Parameter type for IterationNumber should be selected as *Iteration Number*-- Parameter type for MaxIterationCount should be selected as *Custom* with integer value which would be max iteration count per login
- Create two functions to decide to invoke login/logout transactions by considering current iteration number and max iteration count per login. Keep these two functions in one header file so that file can be

included in script through global.h. Below is the example of functions to check doLogin/doLogout--To check Login

```
int checkDoLogin()
]{
    if(atoi(lr_eval_string("{IterationNumber}")) % atoi(lr_eval_string("{MaxIterationCount}")) ==1)
]   {
        return 1;
    }
    else
]   {
        return 0;
    }
-}
```

LR Parameter for Iteration
Number and max ietration count
per login

--To check Logout

```
int checkDoLogout()
{
    if(atoi(lr_eval_string("{IterationNumber}")) % atoi(lr_eval_string("{MaxIterationCount}")) ==0)
    {
        return 1;
    }
    else
    {
        return 0;
    }
}
```

- Invoke these two functions to decide to login/logout like below and on that basis invoke respective transactions. Below is the example

```
doLogin = checkDoLogin();
doLogout = checkDoLogout();

if(doLogin ==1)
{
    xcmLogin();
}

if(doLogout ==1)
{
    xcmLogout();
}
```

- To work reduce login properly, "Simulate a new user on each iteration" setting should be disabled for browser emulation in runtime setting

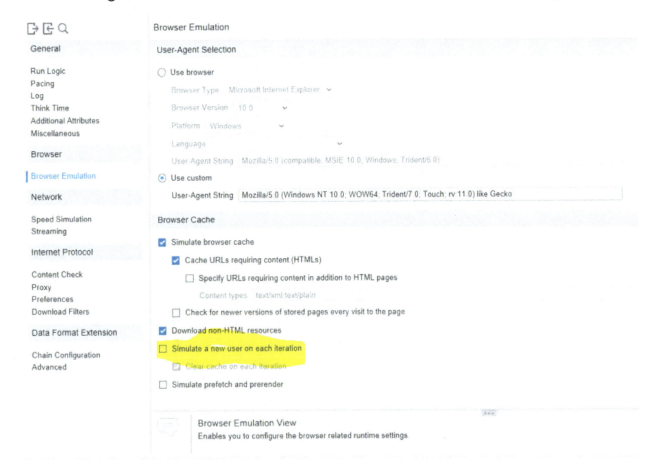

MODULAR APPROACH IN LOADRUNNER SCRIPTING

NEED OF MODULAR APPROACH:

Modular approach is implemented in scripts to avoid write/update same code at many places. Common functionalities are written in one place and can use them in different scripts. Suppose there are four scripts for any project with same login, home page requests. Why to write these common areas multiples times in all scripts? This automatically reduces the time to update scripts with no errors/mistakes.

IMPLEMENTATION:

- Write common code/actions in header file. Each action should have separate function so it can be accessible whenever required
  - CommonActions.h file could have functions for Login and Logout user actions
  - Other user actions can be place in different file
- Place these header files outside of the script folder so it can be accessible through other scripts as well
  - If you are running test from Performance Center, then place these files on common shared location soall load generators can access files. You can keep files on controller and use shared location path
- Add code in globals.h to include common header files from location where you kept all common headerfiles, like below

```
MakeLeaveEntry_XS : globals.h ×    MakeLe...veEntry_XS : Runtime Setti...    MakeLea

1    #ifndef _GLOBALS_H
2    #define _GLOBALS_H
3
4    //----------------------------------------------------------------
5    // Include Files
6    #include "lrun.h"
7    #include "web_api.h"
8    #include "lrw_custom_body.h"
9    #include "C:\\A3Equipo\\LoadTest_Solution\\CommonActions.h"
10   #include "C:\\A3Equipo\\LoadTest_Solution\\CreateLeaveEntry.h"
11   //----------------------------------------------------------------
12   // Global Variables
13
14   #endif // _GLOBALS_H
15
```

- Include required actions in script from these common files by invoking respective methods, for example,
  - MakeLeaveEntry_XS script contains 3 actions, Login, CreateLeaveEntry and Logout. So invokedrespective functions in each action like below,

- A3Equipo_Login() function invoked from CommonActions.h header file which contains user actions forLaunch and login with their respective transactions

```
MakeLeaveEntry_XS : Login.c ×

1   Login()
2   {
3       A3Equipo_Login();
4       return 0;
5   }
6
```

- A3Equipo_CreateLeaveEntry() function invoked from CreateLeaveEntry.h header file which contains all remaining Business transactions to complete user workflow

```
MakeLeaveEntry_XS : CreateLeave... ×

1   CreateLeaveEntry()
2   {
3       A3Equipo_CreateLeaveEntry();
4       return 0;
5   }
6
```

- A3Equipo_Logout() function invoked from CommonActions.h header file which contains user actions for Logout with their respective transactions

```
MakeLeaveEntry_XS : Logout.c ×

1   Logout()
2   {
3       A3Equipo_Logout();
4       return 0;
5   }
```

Transaction Structure:

Business Transaction

Business transaction name should have some prefix to identify and filter records from analyzer, therefore name could be like

BT_ScenarioPrefix_FirmType_TransactionNumber_NameOfBT

Implementation

- Define LR variable in Vuser_Init to store ScenarioPRefix, FirmType/ClientType details like,lr_save_string("XS", "ClientType");lr_save_string("MLE", "ScenarioPrepix");
- Use these variables for business transaction prefix like, lr_start_transaction(lr_eval_string("BT_{ScenarioPrepix}{*ClientType*}{TransactionNumber}_SelectEmpresa"));

Request Transaction

- Request Transaction name should be - RT_ScenarioPrefix_FirmType_TransactionNumber_RequestMethod_RequestURL

Implementation

- Tool implemented to add sub transaction to request in script
- Location of script need to be taken from the shared location where scripts are maintained. You need to get latest code from here and run it
- Select script file where you want to add Sub transactions and click on Add Sub Transaction button. Transactions will get added to your selected script

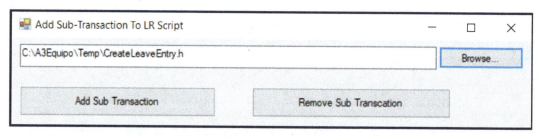

- Right now, Remove Sub Transaction code has not implemented so take backup of your script file before adding sub transaction

Note –

- Reduce use of C variables and pointers to avoid **Out of Memory issue**

Scripting – Apache JMeter

When it comes to scripting in JMeter, there are various techniques and features that a person can consume to create effective and efficient test scripts. Here are some commonly used JMeter scripting techniques:

- Recording: JMeter provides a built-in HTTP(S) Test Script Recorder that allows you to record the interactions between your web application and the browser. By configuring the browser to use JMeter as a proxy, you can capture the requests and responses, which can be used as the basis for your test script. This technique is useful for quickly creating a script by capturing user interactions.

- Manual Scripting: If you prefer to create test scripts manually, you can add elements to your test plan one by one. JMeter provides a wide range of elements, such as samplers (HTTP Request, JDBC Request, FTP Request), configuration elements (HTTP Cookie Manager, HTTP Header Manager), and listeners (View Results Tree, Aggregate Report). You can add these elements to simulate user actions and configure the necessary settings manually.

- Parameterization: Parameterization is an important scripting technique in JMeter. It involves replacing hard-coded values in your test script with variables that can be dynamically changed during test execution. This allows you to simulate different user inputs or data sets. JMeter provides variables, CSV data sets, and functions that you can use for parameterization.

- Correlation: In scenarios where the server returns dynamic values (e.g., session IDs, tokens), you need to correlate those values to maintain the integrity of your script. Correlation involves capturing the dynamic values from previous server responses and reusing them in subsequent requests. JMeter provides Regular Expression Extractor, XPath Extractor, and JSON Extractor elements that can help extract and store dynamic values for correlation.

- Test Fragments: Test Fragments are reusable modules that can be included in multiple test plans. They allow you to define common test elements, such as HTTP requests, configuration settings, or assertions, and reuse them across different test scenarios. Test Fragments help in maintaining modular and reusable test scripts.

- Timers: Timers are used to introduce delays between requests, simulating think times or pacing between user actions. JMeter provides various timers, such as Constant Timer, Gaussian Random Timer, or Uniform Random Timer. Timers help in emulating realistic user behavior by introducing pauses between requests.

- Pre- and Post-processors: JMeter provides pre- and post-processors that allow you to modify request or response data before or after they are sent or received. You can extract data from responses, manipulate variables, or add additional information to requests using these processors. Pre- and post-processors help in preparing test data or extracting data for analysis.

- Script Enhancers: JMeter provides several features and functions that can enhance your test scripts. For example, you can use timers to introduce delays between requests, post-processors to manipulate response data, or pre-processors to modify request data. You can also use JMeter functions, such as __setProperty and __getProperty, to set and get properties during test execution.

- Controller Types: JMeter provides various types of controllers to control the flow of the test plan. For example, the Loop Controller allows you to repeat a set of requests a certain number of times, while the If Controller enables you to execute specific requests based on certain conditions. These controllers help you create complex test scenarios and control the flow of your test execution.

- Test Logic and Flow Control: JMeter offers various controllers and logic elements to control the flow of your test plan. You can use If Controllers to define conditional behavior based on certain conditions, Loop Controllers to repeat a set of requests, and Random Controllers to execute requests randomly. These elements enable you to simulate realistic user behavior and handle complex test scenarios.

- Assertions: Assertions are used to verify the correctness of server responses. By adding assertions to your test plan, you can check for specific patterns, verify response codes, or validate the presence of certain elements. JMeter provides multiple assertion elements, such as Response Assertion, Duration Assertion, and XPath Assertion, which you can use to validate the expected behavior of your application.

Business Transaction

The JMeter Transaction Controller can be a very handy tool for organizing different segments of your test and determining how those segments will appear in a report. The Transaction Controller generates an additional sample which measures the overall time taken to perform the nested test elements

IMPLEMENTATION:

If you want to create a script using Jmeter, then for the first step you need to install Apache JMeter on your system.

1. Open Apache Jmeter.

2. In Workbench, add 'HTTP(S) Test Script Recorder'.

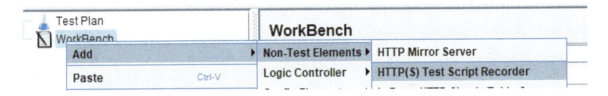

3. Add Thread Group in Test Plan.

4. Add Recording Controller in Thread Group.

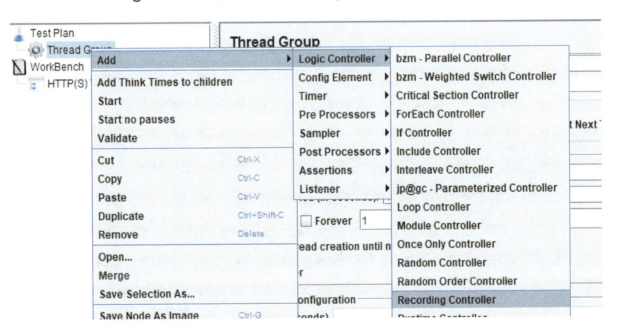

5. Go to 'HTTP(S) Test Script Recorder' and set Target Controller.

6. Click on Start button.

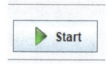

7. It starts recording. You can continue recording until the task is accomplished.

8. Add other test element in Test Plan and your initial script is ready, now a person needs to apply techniques mentioned above to customize the script to simulate end user experience

MODULAR APPROACH IN JMETER SCRIPTING

Modularization plays a crucial role in effective automation by dividing your application into smaller, isolated tests that can be reused in larger, more complex tests. An example of suitable modularization candidates includes activities like logging in, logging out, and high-volume journeys through your application, such as search functionality.

The reason behind adopting this approach is that when these commonly used and high-volume functional activities undergo changes, you only need to update a single test instead of multiple tests. If a particular business functionality is used only once in a single script, there is no need to modularize it. However, if it is utilized multiple times, it is advisable to consider modularization.

JMeter allows you to modularize your test scripts using Test Fragments. By creating reusable Test Fragments, you can build complex test scenarios in a more organized and maintainable manner. Test Fragments can be shared across multiple test plans, allowing you to reuse common test elements and reduce redundancy.

We could use this in a more complicated test, if we had a set of 3 tests that:

Test 1 (add-new)	Test 2 (update-existing)	Test 3 (delete-existing)

• Logged on • Added a new item • Logged off	• Logged on • Search for item • Update existing item • Logged off	• Logged on • Search for item • Deleted item • Logged off

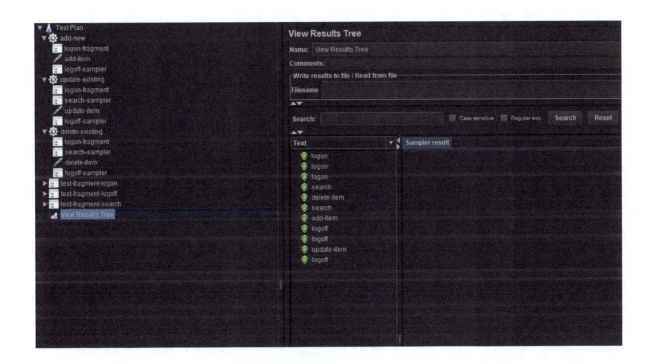

In nutshell, this is the benefit of modularization (screenshot below), if you consider a much more complicate test suite with a lot of tests and a change was made to an aspect of the application under test with a modularized approach the scripting rework is kept to a minimum.

Chapter XI

Performance Testing Types/Methodologies

There are several types of Performance Testing Types or Methodologies that you can apply to the application under test based on the desired outcome you anticipate or expect. As a tester you must anticipate and project what test outcome would be and to get that outcome how you should be testing the

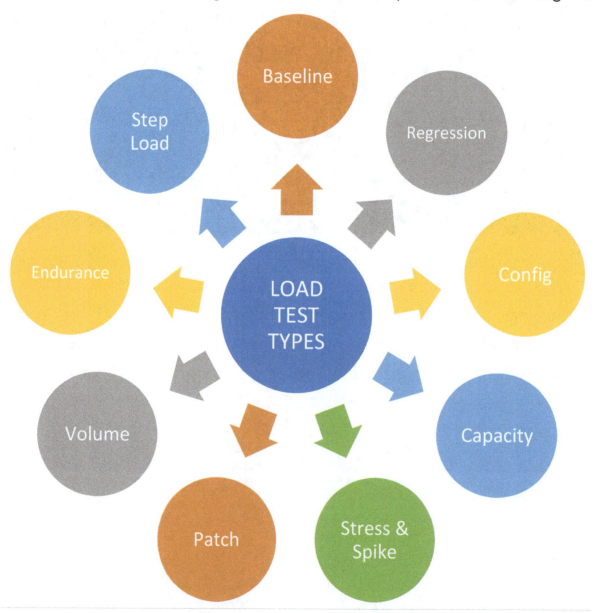

application and infrastructure. You may also need to choose multiple types and methods to obtain the objective. These different methods are described in detail below.

Baseline Load Testing

While determining the application and Infrastructure performance for the first

time is being referred to as Baselining the application performance and called as Baseline Testing. Usually even if there is a major change in infrastructure or architecture of the application, the baselines are repeated. Baseline testing is the first step to understand Application  performance and infrastructure behavior for a desired load level that would then be compared with any code or infrastructure configuration changes for concluding on the change made

Regression Testing

Usually, Performance Testing is not a one-time activity on the application or infrastructure under test. It's a recursive practice that is being performance or recommended to be performed for major releases, code changes,

infrastructure configuration changes as well as any feature addition. Once the baseline is done, keeping the test parameter same, the test is repeated on these changes (one change at a time is recommended to avoid variables to compare against) which is referred to as Regression Testing. Any performance change in a negative sense

observed due to the change tested is marked as Performance or Scalability Issue/Bug/Defect. These defects when further re-tested also referred to as a regression testing. The term is very similar to a Bug/Defect Regression testing that is done during Automation or Manual test cycles, however, with a major differentiator that, it is not always regressed for a Defect but also for a code/infrastructure change or to an extent a build or release change.

Patch Testing

As Performance Testing should be done regressively for build changes or release changes following the sprint cycle with the development team, sometimes the fix to a performance issue is being provided early within the sprints. To test these fixes, a patch is applied to the

load test environment, so the test carried out to regress the issue with the applied patch is referred as Patch Testing. Patch could be of any type, a change in code or a change in Database script or Store procedure in a way that it can easily be applied to the environment without redeployment of the entire build.

Configuration Testing

In a situation where the Performance issue is observed at infrastructure level and stakeholders believe it to be a configuration problem that required to be changed, Configuration test is performed. These tests are also performed to determine the optimum configuration or SKU of

infrastructure resources. For DB server, configurations like MaxDOP setting, various Trace Flags changes, Temp file configuration changes, etc., has also been categorized in this type of testing methodology. All such changes are also recommended to be tested independently to understand performance impact of such changes and its performance gain. With the change in infrastructure provider like Cloud, various configuration for scaling and autoscaling techniques are also load tested and referred in this category.

Capacity Test

Once a Baseline is performed, tests that are taken to determine limiting factors of application and its infrastructure components are referred to as Capacity Test. Majority of the time tests are taken to identify or determine user load capacity, however, there would also be a need to determine capacity of each infrastructure components to build capacity model. Capacity model is created by studying behavior of each infrastructure components when they are stressed to

their limits to determine their capacity and breaking point to identify load or throughput suppodrted. These numbers are then plugged together into a calculation to obtain resources required by an application for desired user or transaction load throughout the year or for a specific peak.

Stress & Spike Test

Load testing an application infrastructure beyond its capacity to study its behavior is referred as Stress Testing. Stress Testing is performed to check infrastructure capabilities and ways to recover the infrastructure. This type of test is carried out to determine application and infrastructure resiliency to identify how soon application and infrastructure

recovers from a saturated and errored state back to normal.

Spike testing is majorly done to determine application and infrastructure response to sudden burst of concurrent load on the system. This is an ad hoc type of testing. Understanding of changing usage pattern is required to plan Spike test. Spike test is more like a scenario creation that come once a while; however, it helps in planning infrastructure components that can handle the behavior of application during those situations

Volume Testing

Volume testing is to identify behavior of application for changing data volume. For a Database sensitive application, application responsiveness depends a lot on its data volume. Such applications are required to be tested for multiple set of

datasets that has anticipated and projected data growth. Volume testing is mainly a future looking testing, and it is very important that data growth is precisely projected

Step Load Test

Step load testing is performed to identify breaking point and Capacity point of

an application. Users are gradually increased in the form of steps. At each level, the load is maintained for definite time and again a step of load is increased. Test identifies where maximum limits are of the application before breaking. Step load test helps in identifying infrastructure requirements for any anticipated user load. In addition to this, it also helps in determining or modelling out infrastructure changes required for seasonal applications

Endurance Test OR Longevity Test OR Soak Test

One of the very important objectives to do performance or load test is to determine infrastructure and its components stability and reliability which can be achieved through performing Endurance test. Endurance test or Soak test is a long duration test or combination of continuous tests for a longer period to keep steady load on the infrastructure and observe its behavior for any anomalies and performance issues.

For planning an Endurance test, the most important aspect is the length of the test that could vary for each application and should be considered based on application's deployment architecture, infrastructure cycling period, usage pattern and scheduled jobs. All these parameters or any other known parameter that could affect the test should be marked for its anticipated outcome.

Usually, Endurance tests are planned and taken to observe memory leak, however, with the cloud platform dynamics, these tests should also be planned to determine scaling configurations, Disks requirements and to determine optimum DB configurations.

Chapter XII

Execution Techniques

Tools available in the market provide various execution techniques that can be used to simulate different scenarios and analyze the performance of your system. Here are some commonly used execution techniques while conducting load test.

Local/Single Machine/Environment

Running a load test on your local machine in allows you to test the performance and scalability of your application in a controlled environment. It is recommended to conduct smaller scale load tests on your local machine before running larger tests on remote load generators or cloud-based solutions. Running a load test on your local machine offers several advantages:

Cost-Efficiency

Running load tests on your local machine eliminates the need to invest in additional infrastructure or cloud-based load testing services. It reduces the associated costs of provisioning and maintaining load generators.

Control and Isolation

By running load tests locally, you have complete control over the testing environment. You can isolate the load generator and the application under test, ensuring that the test results are not influenced by external factors or network fluctuations.

Test Iteration and Debugging

Local load testing enables quick iteration and debugging of test scripts and scenarios. It allows you to easily make changes to your test script, runtime settings, or scenario design and observe the results immediately, without the need for complex setup or coordination.

Realistic Performance Evaluation

Load tests run on local machines can provide a realistic evaluation of the application's performance in the specific environment where it will be deployed. It allows you to assess how the application performs under load on the actual hardware and network conditions that will be encountered by end-users.

Security and Data Privacy

For applications that handle sensitive or confidential data, running load tests on a local machine can ensure data privacy and security. It eliminates concerns about exposing sensitive information to external load testing services or the cloud.

Resource Utilization

Local load testing allows you to fully utilize the available resources of your local machine, such as CPU, memory, and network bandwidth. This can provide a more accurate representation of the application's performance under load, as it leverages the capabilities of your hardware.

Collaboration and Development

Running load tests locally facilitates collaboration within development teams. Developers and performance engineers can work closely together to analyze the test results, identify performance issues, and make necessary code or configuration changes in real-time

While running load tests on local machines has its advantages, it's important to note that it may have limitations in terms of scalability and the ability to simulate larger loads. In such cases, it may be necessary to consider distributed load testing or cloud-based load testing solutions.

Distributed Testing

This technique allows you to distribute the load across multiple machines to simulate real-life situations and effectively measure the performance of your application. You can conduct a load test using the Controller and Agent approach. The Controller acts as the central hub for managing the load test, while the Agents generate the load by simulating virtual users. This technique allows you to distribute the load across multiple machines, simulating a higher number of concurrent users and increasing the test capacity.

Scalability

Distributed testing allows you to distribute the load across multiple load generators or agents. This enables you to simulate a large number of virtual users and generate high loads that may not be feasible with a single local machine. It provides scalability to handle heavy loads and evaluate the application's performance under realistic conditions.

Resource Utilization

By leveraging multiple load generators or agents, distributed testing maximizes resource utilization. Each load generator or agent can simulate multiple virtual users, utilizing the available CPU, memory, and network resources efficiently. This enables you to generate a higher load without overburdening a single machine.

Realistic Load Generation

Distributed testing more accurately simulates real-world scenarios by distributing the load across multiple machines. It allows you to mimic the behavior of geographically distributed users, ensuring that the application's performance is assessed under diverse conditions.

Enhanced Performance Monitoring

With a controller-agent architecture, you can centrally monitor and control the load test execution from the controller machine. This provides real-time visibility into the performance metrics, including response times, throughput, and errors, across all the load generators or agents. It simplifies the analysis of test results and facilitates quick identification of performance issues.

Simultaneous Testing of Multiple Scenarios

Using a controller-agent setup, you can run multiple load test scenarios simultaneously, each with its own set of load generators or agents. This allows you to compare the performance of different scenarios or test variations, making it easier to identify the most optimal configuration for your application.

Load Generator Distribution

Distributed testing enables you to distribute the load generators or agents geographically, closer to the target users or application servers. This helps assess the application's performance from different locations, considering network latency and geographical variations that can impact user experience.

Load Balancing

In a distributed testing environment, load balancing techniques can be employed to evenly distribute the load among the load generators or agents. This ensures that each load generator or agent

shares an equal portion of the load, preventing any single machine from becoming a performance bottleneck.

Overall, distributed testing or a controller-agent architecture provides the flexibility, scalability, and enhanced performance monitoring capabilities necessary to conduct comprehensive load testing and accurately evaluate an application's performance under various conditions, this is recommended to be used for testing large-scale applications.

Cloud Testing

Cloud load Testing provides a scalable and flexible platform for load testing using cloud capabilities. It allows you to simulate realistic load scenarios and evaluate the performance of your applications under different conditions. The exact steps and configurations may vary depending on your specific requirements and the load testing tools you choose to use, this offers several advantages below

Scalability

Cloud testing allows you to easily scale up or down the load generation capacity based on your testing needs. Cloud platforms offer on-demand resources, enabling you to simulate a large number of virtual users and generate significant loads without the need for extensive infrastructure setup or provisioning.

Global Availability

Cloud testing services are available in various regions around the world. This enables you to distribute the load across different geographical locations and simulate user traffic from diverse regions. It allows you to evaluate the application's performance under different network conditions and ensure optimal user experience for users across the globe.

designed by **freepik**

Cost-Efficiency

Cloud testing eliminates the need to invest in and maintain dedicated infrastructure for load testing. You pay for the resources you use during the test, avoiding the upfront costs associated with purchasing and managing load generators or agents. Additionally, you have the flexibility to scale resources up or down as needed, optimizing costs based on your testing requirements.

Elasticity

Cloud platforms provide the ability to dynamically adjust the load generation capacity during the test. This elasticity allows you to quickly increase or decrease the number of virtual users or load generators based on the test scenario. It enables you to simulate realistic load patterns and handle peak loads without any significant delays or manual intervention.

Accessibility and Collaboration

Cloud testing platforms can be accessed remotely, enabling teams to collaborate easily regardless of their physical location. Multiple team members can simultaneously access and monitor the load test results, facilitating collaboration and faster analysis of test data. This enhances teamwork and streamlines the load testing process.

Managed Services

Cloud testing services often provide managed infrastructure and tools, reducing the burden of infrastructure maintenance and management. The cloud provider takes care of provisioning and maintaining the necessary resources, allowing you to focus on designing and executing the load tests effectively.

Realistic Environment

Cloud testing platforms offer a scalable and realistic environment for load testing. They provide a wide range of network configurations, virtual user simulation capabilities, and integrations with various protocols and technologies. This allows you to accurately replicate real-world scenarios and assess the application's performance under different conditions.

Flexibility and Agility

Cloud testing allows you to quickly set up and execute load tests without the need for lengthy infrastructure setup or configuration. You can easily adopt different load testing tools, leverage various testing frameworks, and integrate with other cloud-based services for comprehensive testing. This agility enables faster time to market and quicker iteration cycles.

In a nutshell, cloud testing provides scalability, cost-efficiency, flexibility, and global accessibility, making it a preferred choice when coupled with distributed testing for load testing as it offers the resources and capabilities necessary to conduct robust and realistic load tests while minimizing infrastructure costs and complexities.

To summarize, by using these common execution techniques through available tools, a person can design effective and comprehensive performance tests. By combining these techniques, you can simulate realistic scenarios, analyze performance metrics, and identify bottlenecks in your system.

Chapter XIII

Data to capture

Test results generate a lot of information like Responsiveness, issues and errors, server counters, DB statistics and data from monitoring tool(s). Analysis is done consolidating all this data together and connecting dots between them

Data should be captured at all layers such that it should help in concluding the results for e.g., Client/Front layer information, gateways/load balancing, web/app server profiling, DB connections to DB profiling and stats.

Executing a test could be as simple as scheduling some scripts and walking away, or it could be much more involved. Different tests can require different levels of interaction. Sometimes you might need to manually intervene during the test (clearing a file or log, kicking off additional scripts, or actively

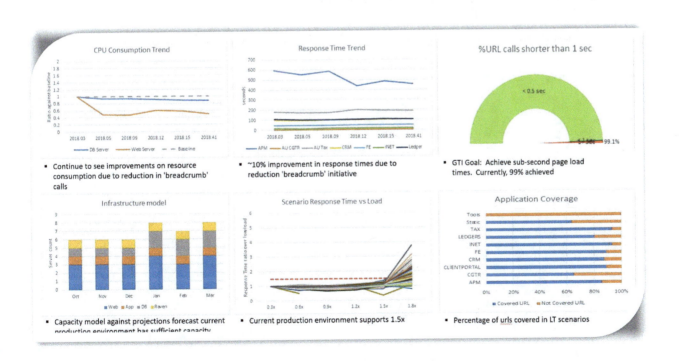

monitoring something), or you might just want to measure something manually using "wall-clock" time while the system is under load.

While tests are running, it can be helpful to monitor their execution. If there's a problem, it would be good to end the test run early and start it up again without having to reschedule execution. It can also be useful to watch streaming application logs, performance test data usage, and performance monitoring applications and utilities.

Once a test execution is complete, data gathering begins. Download test logs from performance tool, application and database logs and export data from monitoring tools for the time test ran, as well as any other data or information that helps with analysis. Save a snapshot of the data before you start to manipulate it. That way you can always go back to the original if you mess something up.

Before you get to far into your analysis, make sure you do a quick scan to make sure all your data passes your heuristics for a successful run. A little debugging and high-level troubleshooting should help you figure out what went wrong. Most often, you'll need to make a small change and re-run the entire test

Chapter XIV

Analytical Techniques

Analysis is a key to Performance testing. There is a huge amount of information or data that gets generated or collected as a part of the process from various sources like Load test tool, Performance Monitoring logs from servers, Application Performance Monitoring (APM) Tools setup on servers, Server IIS Logs or data from log analytics, Data base performance and profiling statistics, Disk and Network statistics, etc. All this information needs to be studied

together in a combination to draw a conclusive theory supporting the analysis.

Analysis is performed keeping in mind the objective of the test to begin with which further explored into anomalies and issues. Most of the time, single source of information is not sufficient to explain any issue or would not be sufficient to prove analytical conclusions. For the same reasons, all the data from various sources need to be correlated for the period when any performance issue starts to surface. Majorly, the performance issue is caused due to saturation of one or many resources, however, whether the entity is victim or source of the issue needs to be determined by analyzing these data sources.

The important aspect of a detailed analysis is to provide stakeholders with pinpointed reasons of WHY any performance issue is observed and one or many ways HOW that issue can be fixed. Development team, Infrastructure team depends on us or a performance testing team to figure out the root cause as we would have a better visibility and perspective to reproduce an issue and identify possible workable solution that can also be validated against the same setup.

Analysis is like investigation. You need to determine the culprit and recreate the scene or scenario to validate the theory. Once the theory is validated, various solutions need to be tested to find an optimum working solution for observed performance problem. Performance issues are never straight forwards so as the fix. Retesting fix is like a regression test as you would never know if a fix at one place don't create an issue somewhere else. To make sure these are studied well, it is always recommended to consult development team and dev architects in the validation process.

There is no one specific Analytical technique that fits all kind of issues, so the analysis needs to be thought through and planned to take into consideration various executions required for validation. As mentioned earlier, it is always recommended to start with the objective of the test as it provides the direction of analysis. A regular baseline and regression test performance issues are required to be checked for saturation on one or more servers and the cause of the same as, whether the saturation is load driven or server or its components capacity driven. Similarly, for a patch test, analysis drives through the area a patch affects and focuses on those areas, all performance parameters are required to be analyzed. No matter if the patch is a code level patch or a DB script patch, all areas should be checked, and their performances should be compared to conclude on the patch sign off. In a similar manner, a configuration change is analyzed, however, while analyzing any configuration, an optimum configuration is expected to be determined, that would require planning quite a few tests to isolate and conclude on a specific or combination of configurations for a specific application under test. Configuration here could be server SKUs, DB settings, Disk configurations, Network configurations, load balancer algorithms, DB partitioning, etc.

A more detailed analytical techniques are discussed and showcased in another book named – Think Performance by Sagar Deshpande and Jagdish Sonawane. This book has various scenarios, case studies discussed in detailed that would give your perspective of performance testing result analysis across different areas of the application and infrastructure components.

Chapter XV

Preparing a Report

Performance Test Report is a key deliverable for any performance test team as it demonstrates the accuracy of the work. The report is a replica of the team's efforts that has been put together for business to make key decisions. Usually,

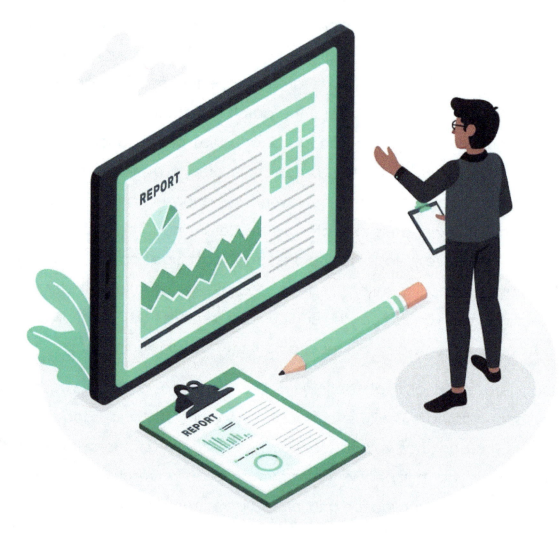

one should take enough time or set an expectation with the stakeholder to get enough time to prepare a complete in-depth test report so that a detailed analytical information can be drafted to prove a theory with supporting information from the data captured using various tools during the test. However, stakeholders would always want to know the results as soon as the test is completed. There will always be a lot of pressure to get preliminary results public. Often this creates a dynamic where the performance tester doesn't want to share results because he doesn't yet understand them and doesn't want people to act on bad data, and a project team demanding results quickly, since performance testing is so critical and occurs so late in the project. As a performance tester, we should always provide the complete information about the test even if it is to be provided without all the supporting data.

We would recommend below steps that can help to provide relevant information to stakeholders in time

> *First, make your raw data available as soon as you get it all pulled together. Get in the habit of publishing the data in a common location (file share, CM tool, SharePoint, wiki, etc.) where at least the technical stakeholders can get to the data they may need to review.*

> *Second, hold a review meeting for the technical team shortly after the run. Hold it after you've done your preliminary checks to see if you even have results worth looking at, but before you do any in-depth analysis. It's at this meeting that you might coordinate a cross-functional team to dig into the logs, errors and response times*

Once you have completed an in-depth analysis and have findings to share, pull them together in a quick document and call together another meeting. Do not provide results without two things:

- A chance to editorialize on the data so people don't draw their own conclusions without understanding the context for the test

- A chance for people to ask questions in real time

There are these two ways you can generate and share the report with stakeholders.

1. Express Report:

A quick report where not all the supporting data from various APM tools are captured together to demonstrate a correlation to prove your theory. This report is drafted by just analyzing the data at the preliminary level. During execution or after the test, the observations can be recorded, and a theory can be drawn to conclude the execution or test. Whether the test is good or bad can be concluded based on the live data and by correlating the data by observations and visualizations of available APM tools. This report can be shared through email or a single page PDF report.

> Note that, in a case when the conclusions cannot be made with the available information and a test may require to be repeated, OR, in certain cases, more analysis is required to be performed. In such scenarios, a report should not be provided, and stakeholders should still be notified about the situations with required information.

2. Formal Report:

In this report all the information should be drafted at a detailed level to showcase the conclusions and its supporting data. A report should clearly state the objective(s) for which the test(s) are taken followed by a conclusion whether those objectives are met or not. It is very crucial to describe in short reasons you think the objectives are met or failed to meet. This first page should give a clear idea to stakeholders on what is going on with the application under load and why. Further, it would always be a good option to talk about Anomalies observed and the issues uncovered during the test. Issues should be documented with the bug management process that the team is following or accepted way to communicate the same with stakeholders. It is always better to isolate the performance bugs with regular manual or automation test bugs either by using tags or a separate category. If these tags and categories are not available, please ask your stakeholders to create the same since it will be easy to triage and regress. Further, your report should include all the information generated by test tool and APM tools corelated together in such a way that it supports each statement you have drafted in your conclusion. If you don't want to look dumb, you should always prove your conclusion with the theory using supporting information in the sequence that is corelated together with respect to timestamp of each data point captured during the test in various tools. In addition to this, it would be recommended that a transaction score card should be prepared that showcases the transaction count alignment as compared to production and performance of those transactions compared to KPIs in a tabular and easily readable format. This information is very useful to understand the performance and to determine areas of the application causing performance issues to focus on. This information also helps for your conclusions and tool data correlation for problem causing transactions and their user action areas to isolate from better performing areas of the application. Finally, do not forget to add Appendix section that should describe in detail your test setup and configuration in addition to Infrastructure details and build or release information. If you have a patch or code change specifically applied to the environment, that should also be mentioned. Appendixes describe the state of your test environment or in other words, Snapshot of your test environment when the test was taken. This type of report should always be shared in a PDF form, on in cases where a confluence or wiki page can be created, one should have that created with all the details. Also, all the supporting data in raw format should be stored at least for 3 build cycles.

To create a good and complete performance test report below tips should be taken into consideration

- In the results, include a summary of the test (model, scenarios, data, etc.), the version/configuration of the application tested, current results and how they trend to the targets, historical results, charts to illustrate key data, and a bulleted summary of findings, recommendations or next steps (if any).

- If (for whatever reason) you can't pull everything together to conclude, send your findings first to key technical stakeholders (DBAs, programmers, infrastructure, etc.) so they can add their analysis and comments. Even this simple step, while slowing things down only a little, may save you hours of heartache from misunderstandings on your part or the part of the reviewers

- Always ask yourself all the WH questions on the final report that you have created to be sent to stakeholders. You will surely improve on the reporting with this approach and your report will always be complete. Try to learn from earlier reporting and avoid getting questions on your report. Less questions means good report.

Chapter XVI

Performance Test Terminologies

Load Test

Load test is used for performing load test on an application. It simulates multiple users as virtual users and executes the test scripts to simulate the real user load on different servers like Application Server, Database server and Web server. Load test can be used with any of the test scripts

Virtual users

Performance Testing Tool generates *the virtual users which simulate the real user's activity*. These are in a real sense are the programming threads who perform the activity on the application/website on the behalf of a real user and generate the load on the server. Several performance testing tools use a different name like VUser, User, Thread, User Load etc .to represent the Virtual User

Think Time

Think time is the time taken between two requests. This can be the time taken by the user to fill a form, view a page or reading some text etc. Think times are used for simulating the real user scenario; how the system will work with a real user

Constant Load

Constant load means same number of users hit the system from the starting of the test till the end. It is like 25 users are using the system for a period of 1hr. All

25 users are hitting the system continuously. This type of testing is mainly used for stress testing

Step Load

In step load, users will join in a step manner. This is the same as different users hitting the system in various times and the number of users in a system is not constant. Following parameter needs to be specified in step load pattern

Start User Count

How many users should hit the system at the time of test start

Step Duration

Time in seconds for the next users to get into the system

Step User Count

Number of users configured to enter the system after every step of the Step load test

Maximum User Count

Maximum number of users that configured to execute the test

Test Mix

Test Mix specifies how different scenarios are executed or used in the system. Different test mixes are formed by studying the system's usage.

For example, if we are doing a load testing on online marketing site; around 60% people will search for different products, 30% will buy few products and 10% bookmark the products. From this usage information, we can form a test mix as 60% simulated users will execute the script for search, 30% will execute the script for buying a product and remaining 10% will execute the script for bookmarking a product

Response time

Most of the Load test is done to understand the response time of an application in given load. If an application is not completed its Load test, then the response time for an expected user load may not be defined.

Response time is the time taken by a transaction to respond to the user. If the response time is very high, the user experience will be low, and the usage of the application may affect it. For decreasing the response time at the same time keeping the rich user interface is one of the challenges

Throughput

Throughput is the number transactions or inputs handled by the server per second. This indicates how much load or requests the server can handle at once. Depends on the throughput and response time requirements we may plan the clustering of servers

Request

A request represents to a URL of a web page. A web page may contain multiple requests belong to the components on the web page like images, javascript, CSS etc. Each component has its own URL.

Transaction

A transaction is a group of requests belong to a particular page. Ideally, each user action has one separate transaction so that response time can be measured individually. Although one transaction can also have multiple user actions. It totally depends on what to measure.

Example: Login Transaction, Search Transaction, Order Submit Transaction etc.

Transactions per second (TPS)

Transactions per second or TPS shows the number of transactions sent by the users in one second. TPS is one of the key metrics of non-functional requirement which helps to set the expected load on the server. The bigger unit of TPS is Transactions per hour (TPH) which represents the transaction rate at an hourly basis.

Iteration

Iteration defines the complete journey of a user mentioned in the test case. It is a group of transactions which denotes the end-to-end flow of the user action.

Example: A iteration can have below transactions:

Home Page -> Login -> Search Item -> Select Item -> Order Item -> Logout

The above iteration represents a user journey from Home Page to Logout.

Iterations per second (IPS)

Iterations per second or IPS shows the number of transactions sent by the users in one second. The iterations per hour or IPH represents the hourly rate of iteration.

Example: If a performance tester conducts the testing for order submission on an e-commerce website and wants to know the total number of orders submitted during the test then he can simply check the number of iterations figure, provided that one order was submitted in one transaction.

Pacing

Just like think time defines a delay between two transactions, *Pacing defines a delay between two iterations*. Pacing helps to achieve the required TPS (transactions per second) in a performance test.

Network Latency

Network Latency represents *the time taken by the network to transfer the data from one end to another.* A channel or network adds some delay while transferring the data between Client and Server. The faster a network, the lesser network latency. Therefore, network latency plays an important role in performance testing.

Server Response Time

Once a request reaches from the client to the server then server takes some time to process the request and respond back to the client. Server Response Time denotes the time taken by the server to process the request.

The sum of network latency and server response time provides the overall response time.

Resource Utilization

Resource utilization includes the servers' processor, memory and network utilizations. How much the application utilizing the server resources determine, whether we can go with a single server or need to have multiple servers or not.

These are three major terms or measures we use in Load test. Apart from these measures, we have network time, latency time, request time, test mix, load mix etc.

Performance Counters

Performance counters are resource utilization information of web/app/DB server which can be captured using multiple tools along with a windows provided tool called "Perfmon". You have to setup different counter set depending on the application type you are testing

Closing Thoughts

Mastering Performance Testing for Success

In this comprehensive guide, we have delved into the fundamentals of performance testing, covering the essential aspects that form the backbone of this crucial discipline and majorly focused on the basics of Performance Testing and provided the perspective of Why it is done, What needs to be covered, When it should be incorporated in the process as part of testing and How it should be done in a right way. We also touched based on Analysis and Reporting results, however, Analysis itself is a huge topic. Analysis is usually not straight forward for any performance tester as the approach and thought process varies based on the application and kind of issues observed. We have seen a lot of performance issues, though similar, but with a completely different cause and impact. Analysis needs an in-depth knowledge of application, its architecture and a logical explanation or a theory that need to be proved using the information available.

As we conclude this book, we would like to express our gratitude for your commitment to learning and improving your skills in performance testing. Remember that practice and continuous learning are essential to becoming a proficient performance tester. Looking ahead, we are excited to announce our forthcoming book which marks the next installment in the performance trilogy, *"Performance Analysis Unleashed – Think Performance"* in this next installment, we would delve deeper into the realm of performance analysis, providing you a wide range topic with examples, approach and recommendations to build your analytical skills in performance testing. Stay tuned for an in-depth exploration journey on this critical aspect of performance testing.

Thank you for joining us on this journey from the novice to expert performance testing. We hope this book has equipped you with knowledge and confidence to tackle performance challenges and drive excellence in your testing endeavors.

Sagar Deshpande

Sagar Tambade

www.ingramcontent.com/pod-product-compliance
Lightning Source LLC
LaVergne TN
LVHW081800050326
832903LV00027B/2030